P9-CCL-165

Mia Marconi has an Italian father and an Irish mother. She grew up in London and has been a foster carer here for over 20 years. During that time she has welcomed more than 250 children into her home. To protect the identities of people she is writing under a pseudonym.

Also by Mia Marconi:

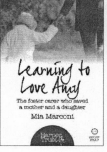

Little Girl Lost

Little Girl Lost

The true story of a broken child

Mia Marconi

with Sally Beck

Certain details in this story, including names, places and dates, have been changed to protect the family's privacy.

HarperTrueLife
An imprint of HarperCollins*Publishers*
1 London Bridge Street
London SE1 9GF

www.harpertrue.com
www.harpercollins.co.uk

First published by HarperTrueLife 2015

1 3 5 7 9 10 8 6 4 2

© Mia Marconi and Sally Beck 2015

Mia Marconi and Sally Beck assert the moral right to be identified as the authors of this work

A catalogue record of this book is available from the British Library

ISBN: 978-0-00-810515-0

All rights reserved. No part of this publication may be reproduced, stored in a retrieval system, or transmitted, in any form or by any means, electronic, mechanical, photocopying, recording or otherwise, without the prior written permission of the publishers.

Chapter One

I've always said that giving birth to a child does not make you a mother and simply fathering a child does not make you a father. What makes you a mother and a father is what comes next: sitting up all night with your little one while they're fighting a fever; watching *The Lion King* on a loop; covering the kitchen with poster paint, sticky tape and cake mix; and endless visits to the park to swing your beautiful son or daughter on the same swing and slide them down the same slide. It's repetitive and, dare I say it, occasionally boring, but that contact with your child makes them feel loved and valued. It's called unconditional love, not childcare. But over the years I had begun to realise that not all parents are capable of loving their children, and that those children who enter the world cocooned by the love of their mother and father are the lucky ones.

Kira initially came to live with us for respite care, and she was a child who could not comprehend the meaning of the word 'love'. Kira could have written a doctorate on rejection, but love was a mystery to her.

She came into our home one Friday night. When you work on the frontline in foster care you very quickly realise that the most urgent calls come on a Friday, usually just as you're about to head out of the door to take your other kids somewhere, or as you're snuggling up in bed with a good book. There's something about having to face the weekend with a demanding child that galvanises people into action.

On this particular Friday I was trying to make dinner, surrounded by chaos. My own five children were demob-happy and already getting into the weekend spirit. 'Mum, I can't find my football shorts,' shouted Alfie. 'Mum, Ruby's got my favourite pyjamas.' 'No I haven't, she's got mine!' 'Mum, Jack's eating my slippers. Mum!' Sleepovers were being planned and sporting activities discussed at top volume as usual, but through the noise I somehow heard the phone ring.

I picked it up. 'Can you hear me?' said a calm, professional voice that sounded vaguely like a social worker. I couldn't, and took the phone into my quiet room, one that the children knew to stay out of. It was my room, peaceful, with warm red walls and a thick fluffy carpet, and as soon as I entered it I felt instantly peaceful. 'Sorry, I can now.'

'We need an emergency placement for the week. It's respite for another set of carers. One of the carers has been in an accident. She's broken her hip and is struggling to cope. Can you help?'

'How old is the poor little mite? And are we her only option?' I said, playing for time. As much as I wanted to help, all our weekend plans would take time to change and I had to be sure I could change them before I committed.

'Kira is three,' she said. 'I'm afraid you are the only option. She hasn't been with these carers for long and she's only just come into care, so obviously this is all incredibly disorientating for her. She can't cope as they are in the midst of a crisis. She is quite needy and her behaviour can be challenging, and the carers are struggling with her. They say she's being quite difficult.'

My mind was racing. From what she had said, I knew that Kira would need one hundred per cent of my attention, and I wondered how I would juggle everything I had to do and give her the care that she needed.

'Please,' said the desperate voice on the end of the phone.

'Okay,' I said. I love little girls anyway and I couldn't say no to a three-year-old in need. I heard the social worker breathe a sigh of relief. She sounded so relieved, in fact, that she was close to tears. 'How long will you be?' I asked.

'About an hour. Is that okay?'

'Fine. See you soon.'

I opened the door of my peaceful, warm red room and stepped back into the chaos. 'Right, kids! I have an announcement to make. We have a little girl staying with us for the week. Her name is Kira and she's three.'

'Does she like Barbie?' Ruby and Isabella said immediately. Francesca pulled a face. 'I hate Barbie,' she said.

'I don't know what she likes yet, but I'm sure she'll love Barbie, and bike rides,' I added, looking at Francesca, who was the tomboy of the two.

In the meantime everyone was hungry, so while they continued asking questions I gave them fish fingers and chips, a Friday night favourite, and cups half full of Robinson's orange squash. I had learnt over the years to fill their cups only half full as more often than not they got knocked over and the contents would end up swimming around their dinner plates. Half-full cups offered damage limitation.

It was early December and unusually cold. The night was bitter and bleak, and just looking out of the window made me shiver. I could tell that snow was fast approaching; you could smell it in the air.

After we'd eaten, my four kids got on with their homework and I tackled the dishes. I looked at them, aged between four and fourteen, and smiled. Martin was helping Alfie, who was still looking for his football strip, while his twin Isabella was tackling a large colouring book. Francesca and Ruby, who were thirteen and fourteen, were discussing what to wear to a party the following night. Everyone was chatting and laughing, and for a change there was no bickering. I smiled again. Our activities that night were just straightforward family routine, which as a parent you take for granted, but when you look back you realise how special those moments were when you were all together and just enjoying each other's company.

A little while later the children heard a car pull up outside the house, and they scampered to the front door like excited puppies, tripping over each other as they went. I followed them, and as I opened it a blast of frosty air hit me full in the face. It reminded me that I must turn up the heating and get the extra blankets out of the airing cupboard. Everyone had cosy duvets, but an extra blanket on top made them even cosier.

It was the social worker, and clinging to her neck was the smallest, frailest little girl, wrapped in a slightly grubby blue fleece blanket. The blanket hid the colour of her hair and most of her face.

'This is Kira,' the social worker said. 'Kira, this is Mia and you'll be staying with her.' She handed Kira to me, and I unwrapped her blanket and saw a skinny little girl with unruly dark hair, an Asian complexion and angry eyes as dark as thunder. I looked at her clothes. She was dressed in blue jogging bottoms

5

and a Thomas the Tank Engine jumper. I caught the social worker's eye. 'She doesn't like pink,' she said, reading my mind. I smiled at Kira. 'There is no rule that says girls have to like pink,' I said, and she blinked.

In that short cuddle, I could feel that Kira was tense and only just the right side of being a bag of bones. She looked frightened as well as angry, and I didn't blame her, but before I could begin reassuring her Francesca shouted:

'Come on, Kira! Let's see what's in the dressing-up box.'

'Bagsy the princess outfit,' said Ruby.

'Bagsy the pirate outfit,' said Francesca. 'Kira, you can have the cowboy outfit. It's your size.'

The children were so welcoming that I saw the fear disappear from Kira's face. Her look was still cautious, but there was the glimmer of a smile now so I put her down and turned my attention back to the social worker.

I had never met this particular lady. She was frail herself and looked overworked; I already knew she was underpaid – no amount of money could compensate for the tasks you have to carry out in social work. I looked at my watch and it was nine p.m. 'It's an hour and 40 minutes' drive home for me,' she said. 'You need a cup of tea,' I said, but she shook her head and handed me the paperwork to sign, along with a Tesco carrier bag bulging with Kira's clothes.

The bag was not a good sign. I knew her carers were quite well off and could easily have given her a small case, so this meant that either it was so chaotic at their house they had packed her things in a rush, or they didn't care that much about her.

I took the handover papers and the looked-after children papers, signed them and gave them back to her. She pulled her coat around her, and for the second time I heard her breathe a sigh of relief. I felt sad for her and wondered how long it would be before she was burnt out. She got in her car and I never saw her again.

It was three weeks before Christmas when this journey started and I had no inkling then where we were going with it. All I knew was that Kira would be staying with us for a week to give her carers a chance to assess their needs.

I looked at her playing with my kids. There were no tears, no tantrums and, although you might think that I would be grateful for that, I knew it was a sign that Kira was suffering from an attachment disorder. I felt sad for her. I knew this meant she had never bonded with a special adult – which in most cases is mum and dad, and if they're not around other members of the family, and if there is no family foster carers take their place – but she was showing no distress at being separated from her primary care givers, as parents and guardians are officially called. I decided I would work hard to give her a family experience that week, but knew I'd have to be careful not to overwhelm her. It was clear her needs had been pretty much ignored up until now but to suddenly make her the centre of attention would probably panic her.

I picked up Kira's paperwork to see what I could glean from it, but there was essential information only.

I called James and Claire, her official foster carers. James answered. 'Hello, James, I'm Mia and I'm looking after Kira this week. I just wanted you to know that she's arrived safely and we're settling her in.' Just then, Kira walked past in the cowboy outfit. 'Would you like to talk to her?'

'No, thank you. I would normally, but we're struggling here a bit. Can we speak later in the week?

'My wife is in shock,' James explained. 'A car hit her as she walked across a zebra crossing and she's broken her hip quite badly. The doctors aren't sure how long she'll need to recuperate until after they operate. They're operating tomorrow. Kira has been so upset, what with the doctors and ambulances, that it's not fair for her to stay here.'

'Well, don't worry. I'll look after her for you,' I reassured him.

'Thank you, Mia, we really appreciate it.'

I knew brief details about them: they lived in a large house near Clacton in Essex and had a child of their own, but had been unable to have more. They thought fostering would be a way to give their own daughter, Jo, a ready-made sibling. It seemed a shame that they had to face this crisis so early in the placement.

Understandably, Kira was quite clingy and spent most of her time with me in the kitchen. She shied away from any affection and wasn't keen on the dogs, and although she played with my children she didn't immerse herself totally. She held back. 'You alright, darling?' I would ask occasionally.

'Yes,' she'd reply.

'Just ask me if you need anything.' She'd nod. It was all very formal, but I didn't want to crowd her. Even so, I kept a constant eye on her. Each time I checked up on her she seemed to be settling well.

There was a knock on the door at 10 a.m. the following Friday morning. The social worker standing there was Roz, a lovely lady I'd met with various other foster children. I headed straight for the kettle. 'I've got the log of how it went, Roz. Shall we go through it?' I was required to write down detail about Kira's moods. 'She was quiet and quite withdrawn but joined in when she was encouraged.'

'That's a good sign,' Roz said.

I told her about our activities: 'We went to the park, and as a special treat on Saturday we had dinner at Pizza Hut.'

'How was she in public?'

'A bit quiet. She was quite pleased to leave. On Sunday we took a long walk in the woods with the dogs, and came back to a huge roast.' Then I went through the rest of the weeks' activities. 'Kira seemed happy enough,' I said, and I believed it was true.

By that point we noticed Kira standing by the front door, wearing her coat. Awkward doesn't begin to describe that moment, and Roz leant over to me and whispered: 'I think she wants to go.' I was wounded for a split second then quickly reminded myself that it was Kira's needs that were important, not mine. Then Roz said: 'She's probably just been a bit overwhelmed. As there's only one other child where she is it might have been a shock coming into all this chaos.' She smiled. I knew this was just good-natured banter; she didn't really think we lived in chaos.

I was expecting her to say, 'Thanks for helping out, we'll take it from here,' but she surprised me as she went on: 'Would you be prepared to have Kira on a regular respite basis if we need you? I've spoken to her carers and Claire will be in a wheelchair for a couple of months, maybe three. They want Kira to stay with them as she's been with them for a few months already. She found it really hard to settle at first, but she's been making some progress and they don't want to disrupt her unless they really have to.'

'I'll be happy to help if you need me,' I said as I walked over to Kira and picked her up. She looked uncomfortable and gave me a withering look.

I put her down gently and opened the front door. The social worker took Kira's small, limp hand, which she quickly snatched away, and led her down the garden path. 'Bye, Kira,' I said. 'Bye,' she said, but neither of them looked back and neither waved, so I shut the door and took a brief moment to reflect.

I began to mull over what had just happened, and I felt hurt and worried about whether Kira had enjoyed her stay with us. My thoughts were interrupted by the phone ringing so I put the problem to one side. Later, I spoke to the kids and was happy that nothing traumatic had happened to Kira while she was with us. I just put it down to her wanting to be in a more familiar setting.

Life carried on and I had little time to think about Kira again. The truth is, I was just another adult who had come into her life for a short period.

Chapter Two

Christmas was on its way and I love Christmas with all my heart. It's like re-entering my childhood again – Christmas time was when I was at my happiest when I was little. Somehow my parents managed to put aside their differences for a few days and made a supreme effort to get into the spirit of things, and that has always stayed with me.

I decorate my home with two trees, one in the front room and one in my enormous kitchen. I cover the house in fairy lights and make sure I light a log fire at night. I dig out all the Christmas songs. 'Not Nat King Cole again!' Martin will shout from the other room. 'Bing's on next!' I shout back, and I sing along to Bing Crosby and Wizzard while I'm cooking the dinner. I love the smell of Christmas too, particularly mulled wine and mince pies.

I'm no cook. I can handle the basics, but my mum could have been a professional and she makes the best Christmas cake you've ever tasted – rich and moist, but not too heavy, and just the right amount of brandy to bring it alive. I've never had one that could compare and my mouth waters just thinking about it. On Christmas Eve at about 4 p.m., a friend and I race down to the supermarket to pick up any Christmas bargains we can find. 'How many turkeys do you need this year, Mia?'

'Two as usual.'

'Well, hopefully they'll be knocked down in price by now.'

'Fingers crossed.'

I never go away at Christmas and there is usually twenty-plus for Christmas dinner. I always just want to be at home with my family, and with the preparations taking up every spare minute, there was no chance to think of Kira.

Christmas and New Year ended, and the pure volume of traffic had made our house look somewhat sad and tired. I felt a bit like a wilted Christmas tree myself, my sparkle had gone and I was worn out.

It never did snow in December but by January there was so much snow it covered the front door step, and it became impossible to get out of the house. We were all milling around at home waiting for it to thaw, but the kids had plenty of new games and toys to keep them occupied, so everyone was happy.

On 6 January I was in the middle of taking the decorations down and clearing up the debris of the festive season when I heard Francesca shout: 'Mum!' She had picked up the phone, which I had missed ringing as I had been vacuuming. 'It's for you!'

I turned the vacuum off and took the handset from Francesca. 'It's Roz,' a voice said. I was stumped for a minute. 'It's Roz from social services. I collected Kira from you in December,' she said. 'Of course. How are you?'

'I'm fine,' she replied. She went through the niceties, asking how my Christmas had been, but we both knew she hadn't called just for that.

'I'm calling about Kira,' she said. I hadn't thought to ask about Kira because I assumed that, as I hadn't heard anything, her carers were coping and Roz was calling about another child. I was wrong. 'I was wondering if you could have her on a regular respite care basis. We're trying to save her placement but physiotherapy is taking up more time than they expected. Not surprisingly, Kira is being quite demanding and they're struggling a bit.'

I paused, remembering Kira looking at the front door with her coat on, waiting to escape. 'I think it's a good idea if I meet her carers before I make that decision, and we would really need to like each other for this to work,' I said. It's like any relationship that involves children and multiple adults. A child will thrive if they see you getting along with the other adults in their life. Kira needed to see us together so I thought we should organise to meet.

'We can do that,' Roz said. 'Are you free tomorrow?'

'I can be,' I replied.

'Okay. I'll pick you up at nine in the morning and drive to meet James and Claire.'

'Fine. See you then.'

Claire and James were both teachers and their five-bedroom detached house was lovely. James was about fifty and greying at the temples, but he still had a full head of hair. He was average build and smartly dressed in corduroys and a checked shirt. Claire was about forty-five and short. She looked like a stern school teacher, I thought.

They welcomed us with tea – always a good sign, I think – and we sat round their large kitchen table. Kira wasn't there but would be coming back at lunchtime, they said.

Claire explained: 'My hip is taking longer to heal than I thought. My sister can help out with Jo, but because Kira is quite "difficult", my sister doesn't think she can manage both of them.'

'I understand,' I said.

'She's a lovely girl really,' James said, 'but she needs more than we can give her at the moment.' They looked at each other, but I wasn't unduly concerned. I knew that Kira would be struggling and that it would all be coming out in her behaviour. 'If you could take her at weekends we can probably cope during the week,' James added. I liked them, they were honest and I could see that we could work together, so I said, 'Yes. I'd like to take her.'

Just then the doorbell rang and it was Claire's sister with Kira. 'Hello Kira,' I said. 'Do you remember me?' She nodded.

'Mia's going to look after you at weekends while Auntie Claire has her treatment,' James explained. 'Oh,' said Kira, before running upstairs. We all talked for a while then it was time to leave. 'I'll see you at the weekend, Kira,' I called up. 'We'll have some fun. Bring a favourite toy with you.' She didn't answer.

In the car on the way home Roz asked, 'What do you think?'

'Of Kira? I think she has had a hard time.'

'You're right. We need to sit down and go through it all.'

When we got home I went through my calendar and offered her some suitable dates. 'Twelfth of January looks good to me,' I said.

'As well as her background, we need to discuss Kira's day to day routine, her likes and dislikes, and to complete the paperwork,' Roz said.

This preparation is essential because without it you might as well be wearing a blindfold trying to care for a child. In some cases there is very little information available, but in Kira's case there was lots of detail. Roz said that she had been placed on the at-risk register since birth. After I heard that, I knew that Kira would have a desperate story, but I wasn't prepared for just how desperate.

It's a comfort in some ways that when I hear the awful truth about the lives of some of the children I've cared for, I realise that my imagination would never be able to conjure up the horrific tales I hear, even if I tried to imagine the worst thing someone could possibly do to a child. This was certainly the case with Kira.

Roz arrived on 12 January with her face red but healthy-looking from the bitter weather. 'Tea?' I asked.

'Yes, please. Lovely,' she said as she began removing endless layers of clothing. 'You have already met Kira so that makes it a bit easier. There's a lot you don't know about her. I'm sure we don't have all the information but I'll tell you what we have found out so far.'

So over our steaming cups I learned that Kira had come into care six months earlier. She was the product of an affair. The word 'affair' paints a picture of illicit romance, secret meetings and love. But this affair had nothing to do with love, it was just two desperate people looking for affection and having sex. The result was Kira, so calling her a 'love child' was just all wrong;

'Kira's father Hafeez was from Pakistan, a married man with two young sons. To the outside world he was a good man from a close-knit family who worked hard. The family supported each other; although a large part of his family was still in Pakistan, those who were in the UK were all involved. Kira's mother Mary was English and she was also married with children. Her family was far larger and she had eight children altogether. She was blonde and blue-eyed while Hafeez's appearance was typically Asian.' That explained Kira's dark eyes and Asian colouring.

The fact that Mary had eight children was a sign-post in itself. There are only a few reasons why people have large families these days and they are either because they absolutely adore children, they're religious and don't use contraception, or they're chaotic and don't take proper precautions. Quite often chaotic parents start out thinking children will fill a hole in their lives, providing them with love that's missing, but it rarely works out like that.

Mary had grown up in a dysfunctional family herself so had married young to get away, hoping to find the love she had never had at home. But finding happiness was a pipe dream, because no matter how hard she tried neither a partner nor her own chil-dren could fill the void left by her rocky childhood. There would be no fairy-tale ending for Mary, and she found out the hard way that she was never going to be Cinderella and her new husband was no Prince Charming.

'Mary's husband Bob had his own issues,' said Roz. He was violent, he drank and he beat Mary, and before long, alcohol was playing a big role in both their lives. They are very needy individuals and similar in many ways. That was the attraction, but it was a recipe for disaster.'

Neither had ever been parented so they had very little chance of making a success of parenting themselves. They had nothing to give their children other than rejection because that was all they had experienced.

'How many times have we heard this story?' I asked Roz. 'I know,' she said.

We had seen this scenario a hundred times before, and I wondered what and who would eventually fix this destructive cycle in people's lives. I would happily have given up my job as foster carer if someone could have solved this problem. Would I ever see the day when my services as a foster carer would no longer be needed, I wondered. Unlikely, I thought.

'So Mary had an affair with Hafeez?' I asked Roz.

'Yes. And Kira is the result. She was born prematurely, but we're not sure how premature she was because Mary didn't go to any antenatal classes and tried to keep her pregnancy a secret. The hospital estimated that Kira was about five or six weeks early so she spent her first four weeks in an incubator.'

I learnt that those four weeks were the first four weeks of rejection that Kira experienced. Mary rarely went to the hospital so the hospital staff contacted social services. 'She had told the nurses that she was too busy looking after her other children, but they weren't convinced.'

'She probably had a point,' I said.

'I know, but anyway, the nurses discovered that Mary was already known to us, as were the other children in her family.'

After hearing Kira's history, I realised why I felt an affinity with her. The rejection she'd suffered wasn't dissimilar to the rejection my dad had suffered as a young boy. I thought back to how his mother had been cast out by her family after she became pregnant with him, how he'd always thought his grandparents were his parents, how after they died he was sent to live with a mother he'd never known and never knew he had. She rejected him and, years later, when he found his real father, his dad rejected him too. I'd come to realise over the years that part of the reason I wanted to foster children who had families who hurt them was because of my dad. If someone had been prepared to care for him and love him, maybe his life could have been happier.

In Kira's case, the authorities were alerted and the system moved into action. Unfortunately for Kira, it was another three years before she was taken into full-time care. Three long years in which Kira suffered more than any child should ever have to.

Social workers are often blamed for leaving children in their chaotic, abusive families for too long, but the courts play a big part in this decision. Before the courts will act to remove any child from a dysfunctional family, social services have to prove that they have tried everything in their power to help turn that family around.

If drugs and alcohol are a problem for the parents, then rehab is the first port of call, then parenting classes and possibly rehousing the parents. Intervention all takes time, and sometimes it works and at other times it doesn't. It's hard to tell how it will turn out, and if it doesn't work the consequences for any children involved are devastating.

There must be a better way, I thought to myself. Surely there must be a way to tell whether a family is able to turn itself around in less than three years? The first three years in a child's life are so important and if they are messed up, then undoing the damage will be an uphill struggle.

Our childhood is so brief compared with the rest of our lives, I thought. It should be grounded in love and security, laughter and adventure. It should be carefree. But while the courts are deciding the best thing to do, a childhood is slipping away. Once it's gone, it's gone, and you can never get those years back. Losing something so precious should never be taken lightly, I reasoned.

'Kira eventually left the hospital in the arms of her mother, wrapped in a white blanket,' said Roz. 'She hadn't been introduced to Bob yet, and as he is fair-skinned and has blue eyes like Mary, it was always going to be awkward.' So as Mary stared at the little bundle, her look wasn't the loving look a newborn could expect; she was looking at Kira's black hair, Asian complexion and dark, dark eyes. Kira looked nothing like the dad she was about to be introduced to.

'Needless to say, Bob didn't take it well, and went on to sexually abuse Kira. The kindest thing Mary could have done would have been to give Kira up for adoption at birth.'

Roz finished talking. I sighed, unable to hide the sadness I was feeling. 'When would you like me to take her?'

'Can you start this weekend?'

We agreed that, initially, this arrangement would last for six months. That would give Claire the chance at recovery that she needed. So Kira began spending her weekends with us.

Over the weeks, I began to feel uneasy about Claire and James, and although I knew Claire was still recovering, it also felt as though they wanted time to spend on their own with Jo, who was three years older than Kira.

One Sunday evening when I dropped Kira off, I used the bathroom upstairs before I left, and I was about to put my head round Jo's door when I heard a chilling conversation. 'It was so nice without you,' Jo told Kira, who said nothing. 'My aunt cooked a massive dinner on Sunday and we all watched *My*

Fair Lady.' It was one of Kira's favourite films because the heroine, Audrey Hepburn, had dark hair like her. 'I hate you,' Kira shouted, before picking up a cup from Jo's tea set and throwing it at the wall. It broke, obviously, and Jo went running down to her mother, crying: 'I hate Kira! Look what she's done!'

Claire responded harshly: 'Kira, no television for you after tea and you will go straight to bed.' Kira looked sullen and stayed silent. I think she knew better than to answer back. Claire saw my shocked face. 'Sorry, Mia, but she has to learn.' I bit my tongue.

Claire hadn't investigated what had happened to cause Kira to react the way she did, which surprised me. At the time I didn't say anything, because I knew that if I did it might make it worse for Kira, but I also knew that at some stage the problem needed to be addressed.

I saw Kira and Jo arguing over a toy once, like all kids do. 'Give it to me,' Jo said. 'It's my turn,' Kira replied. In that situation I would have said, 'Jo, you play with it for thirty minutes then it's Kira's turn.' But Claire shouted at Kira: 'If you can't play nicely then you can't play at all! Go to your room and don't come out until you're sorry.' Jo looked smug and said, 'Thank you, Mummy. Kira never plays nicely.'

I couldn't say anything to Claire and James, but I couldn't keep quiet anymore and I talked to social services about it, who said they would deal with it.

Not long after that conversation I got a phone call from Roz. 'Claire and James don't think they can cope anymore. They say Kira is being really disruptive. She's smashed up their bathroom. They say she's peed on their wooden floor, and they'll have to have it stripped and polished.'

'Why didn't they just wipe it up with a mop and bucket?' I asked.

'Hmmm. Not sure,' Roz said. 'But worse, they say that Kira is masturbating continuously in front of Jo.'

'It's not behaviour I recognise, Roz.'

'We thought you would have told us if anything like that had happened, but we were wondering if you would take her permanently.'

I didn't hesitate. 'Of course we will,' I said. I had already discussed this possibility with Martin and the family, and they were happy for her to stay permanently. 'Okay, next weekend, is it okay if she moves in?'

'That's fine. Bring her on Friday and I'll have everything ready.'

As I'd clicked with Kira straight away I had no concerns about her living with us. I understood her and hoped I could help her.

Interestingly, Dad formed an instant bond with Kira, presumably because they subconsciously understood each other too. They never talked to each other about the rejection they'd suffered but they instinctively gravitated towards each other. It always amazes me how that happens, how we pick up on unspoken but shared experiences.

Chapter Three

Kira already had a room at our house, but I made sure that I took out anything pink and got her a blue rug, lampshade and Thomas the Tank Engine duvet cover.

James and Claire brought her the following weekend but Jo didn't come. It was an awkward farewell, quite cold, with no hugs. I offered them a cup of tea. 'No, thanks, we should get back,' James said. 'Bye, Kira,' they said. 'Bye,' Kira responded. There was no cuddle, no kiss on the cheek. 'Okay, I'll see you to the door,' I said, and when we were out of Kira's earshot I said, 'Would you like her to call you?'

'No, it's alright,' they said, and left. On Monday, they resigned as foster carers and I can't say I was surprised.

'I hate Jo,' was the first thing Kira said when I walked back into the kitchen. 'I know, darling, but you don't have to see her any more.'

'Good,' she said, and then burst into tears. It was a rare show of emotion for Kira. She never seemed to be frightened, happy or sad.

I got down to her level and gave her a hug. She always stiffened when I put my arms around her, but I still thought it was important and I cuddled her just long enough to get the message across that I cared about her. Kira rarely looked you in the eyes, but as her eyes shifted from left to right I managed to catch her gaze and what I saw in them was anger. I felt so sad and tried to comprehend what she must be feeling.

My heart went out to Kira and I wondered how much more rejection she could take. I hoped it wasn't too late to show her that there were good people in the world, that she was worth something, and that people could love and care for her, but I also had to take on board the fact that she was three, and most of the damage would already be done. I knew I would never be able to heal her completely. I could never replace her parents, but our family would do all we could. It is so hard to repair your soul once you've been rejected by your parents, but I hoped I could help set her on a road where she could find some happiness. It would be a long road even if I could help. I knew that.

She got on really well with Ruby and they had some lovely moments together, but she and Francesca clashed. Francesca wasn't as patient as Ruby and I suspect she was jealous that her younger sister was making friends. This generally happened with one of the children when we had a new foster child in the house. It was natural, the dynamic had changed, but I knew it all settled down in the end.

One of the first things Kira and I did together was make a memory board, or life stories as we call them. It's basically an A3 sheet of paper covered with photographs and written memories, like one big scrapbook. We pasted some photographs of Kira's family onto the blue paper then I wrote what she asked me to. 'This is my mummy, this is my daddy, these are my brothers and sisters. I don't see them. This is Francesca and Ruby but they're not my sisters. I live with Mia now, but she's not my mum and I don't call her Mum.' All this was fine by me. It was important for her to find a way to come to terms with her life as it actually was. There was no glossing over the fact that she'd been dealt a desperate hand and needed to process it somehow. Over the next few months and years, as her life progressed with us, we made lots of memory boards.

To say that Kira wasn't an easy child is an understatement. Even as a three-year-old she was verbally aggressive. 'You silly bitch,' she would say. 'Now that is not the sort of language you should use,' I'd say gently. 'Fuck off!' she'd say.

'Saying "go away" is a much better way to put that. People will get upset if you swear at them.'

'I don't care.'

'Everyone cares what people think about them.'

'Well, I don't.'

I knew she was testing the boundaries with me, and at that stage I would retreat to think of a different way to deal with the situation.

Kira was violent, manipulative, stubborn, introverted and aggravating. She knew how to repel people by swearing at them and being abusive, which just made me more determined to understand her and help her to see that not everyone was a monster. But more than that, I wanted people to see that she was not a monster either. She was just a little girl who had suffered.

I had to admit Kira had many, many problems, and I would need to deal with them all.

'Martin, because of the sexual abuse Kira's experienced, she might behave in a sexualised way when there are men around. She always wants to sit on boys' and men's laps.'

'Okay, love, I'll talk to Alfie.'

Sitting on someone's lap should not be a problem for little children, but when Kira did it, it was not in the same way you would expect a little girl to. She would wriggle around on their genitals, which was obviously quite embarrassing for them. It wasn't long before a family member experienced this and I remember my brother being completely thrown when Kira plonked herself down on his knee one afternoon. He froze as Kira began to move suggestively up against him. He was stunned that a child this young was capable of doing what she was clearly doing. Joe looked at me, confused. 'Kira, can you come and help me with the tea?' I said. And she wriggled off Joe's knee.

Later, we had a private chat and I said in the kindest voice I could, because I didn't want to embarrass her: 'Kira, you shouldn't sit on men. I know your stepfather wanted you to, but it was wrong and you don't have to do it.' She looked blankly at me, but she took it in. She didn't stop immediately, though. She had probably learned that if she didn't she would get a good hiding. I always say the unlearning behaviour is so much harder than learning it, but gradually she came to trust that nothing bad would happen to her if she followed my advice. By the time she was seven her sexualised behaviour was much less noticeable, but it never totally disappeared. Occasionally, she would slip back, but not often enough for me to be concerned, although in times of stress I think she used it to distract people or horrify them so that they would leave her alone.

She regularly threw tantrums and anything could set her off. 'I don't want to go to bed!' she would scream some nights. 'I don't want to go in the bath, I don't want to wash my hair.'

She found social events particularly difficult, especially weddings and parties. It didn't matter whether they were at our house or elsewhere, she would inevitably have a meltdown. Family events made her feel uncomfortable because she felt she didn't belong.

I understood that, we were all strangers and she was only three and tantrums were normal, but Kira's tantrums went beyond what you would expect of a child her age. Plus, once she started a meltdown it was hard to calm her. Her behaviour just made me more determined to get through to her and to prove to her that she could feel safe in these situations.

At parties she would generally punch another child and I'd have to leave. 'Kira, why did you hit Jack?' I'd say.

'Because I don't like him. He looked at me funny.'

'He was just trying to be friendly.'

'Well, I don't want him to be friendly.' She'd never bolt, though, and she didn't hit any of my children. She respected them.

If the party was at home it was no better. She'd flood the bathroom or smash up her bedroom. Once she took her knickers off and started running around so that everyone could see her bare bottom. 'I think it's time we went,' my sister said, to save embarrassment. And within five minutes the whole family had put their coats on and gone home. They weren't angry, they just took the cue.

I learned really quickly to keep her close to me. 'Come and help Mia with the sandwiches,' I'd say to distract her.

'I want to put the cheese in them.'

'You can do that. You're really good at doing that.' I'd watch her body language for tell-tale signs that indicated she was about to do something that would either mean I'd have to leave wherever we were, or that people at our house would be departing prematurely.

I would be walking on eggshells at social occasions, and the minute I saw Kira's eyes darting rapidly around the room and her body stiffen I knew I had to act. A change in body language was a sure sign that she was getting agitated and only havoc could follow. 'Come with me, Kira,' I'd say, and I would try to take her hand to lead her to a safe place. 'Fuck off!' she'd say, before trying to kick me or slap me away.

Somehow I'd manage to get her into a quiet room. I would talk to her gently and try to find something she wanted to do more than socialise. 'Please try not to spoil Francesca's party (or Ruby's, or Christmas dinner, or Martin's birthday …),' I'd say. 'You can hold my hand or stay in here and do some colouring. If you want to sit in your room that's fine or we can read a book.'

Once her anxiety subsided I'd take her back into the gathering, but she never really enjoyed them, unless there was a baby there. The one surprising thing about Kira was that she loved babies. There was never a problem if there was a baby around because Kira would play happily for hours.

Calming her down did get easier though, and after about a year she stopped kicking me when I suggested quiet time somewhere. She would also let me take her hand. The first time she didn't pull away I felt tears of happiness prick my eyes. I was elated but I knew I had to keep myself in check. I also knew that this was a turning point. It was such a small thing but huge in terms of Kira's development. It meant she was beginning to trust me, and for Kira to allow herself to trust any adult was fantastic. It was the first step towards her being able to form stable relationships and it was a step I'd wondered if I'd ever see.

Chapter Four

Kira got a place at the local school when she was four. I hoped this would be a new start for her, but although she was beginning to trust me, she found it impossible to make friends. 'Aggressive' and 'angry' were the words I most heard when the teachers talked to me about her. She was never invited to children's houses or to birthday parties. I tried to help her integrate and often stood in the playground smiling at the other mothers, only to be greeted with blank stares and cold shoulders. If I approached any of them I'd hear, 'Kira upset my daughter,' 'Kira hit my son,' 'Kira swore at my child.' The list was endless. It became easier for me to put my hood up and stand behind the trees while the other mothers bitched about me behind my back. It became so that I felt bullied, and if I was feeling like that I wondered how Kira must be feeling.

At the end of the school day the children would all file out into the playground. Kira was usually the last, accompanied by a teacher. She was last because it was safer, or because more often than not the teacher needed to talk to me.

I could always spot her because she had her eyes glued to the ground. She very rarely looked up, and her forehead was normally covered in bruises from where she had walked into doors, walls or a lamp post.

Each morning I struggled to make her hair look pretty. Making her hair tidy was all about trying to help her develop a sense of pride in her appearance, but after a while I gave up. It usually ended in a drama and it helped neither of us if we arrived at the school gates agitated and flustered.

Kira had the most feminine name but wasn't ready to look like a little girl and, in fact, as the years went on she became more and more of a tomboy.

'I found a denim dress I thought you might like. Come and have a look.' And I'd show her the plainest pinafore I could find online. 'I'm not wearing a dress! Ever! Never! I like tracksuit bottoms and jeans.' So Kira's casual clothes were all about sportswear and trainers. As she dressed like one, you would have thought she might have found friends amongst the boys, but she didn't.

School years never became any easier – far from it. They simply got harder as Kira refused to fit in anywhere, with the girls or the boys. None of them understood her, and why should they. None of them would ever be able to relate to what she'd been through.

In a bid to try to get inside her world I would walk to school at break time and hide behind a tree so that I could watch her interact with the other children. Anyone observing me would have had the right to call the police, but my desperate need to unravel Kira's world had taken over. I watched her for hours as she stood in corners or tried to attract the attention of different groups by kicking them or pulling their hair.

I felt so sad that she was so isolated and couldn't work out how to socialise. I'd watch her standing in the corner, her shoulders slumped and head bowed. I watched as playground assistants tried to encourage her to play with other children or encourage other children to play with her. I'd be willing her: 'Just go and play Kira,' I'd mutter. 'That little girl's being kind.' And I'd watch as another child gave up trying to include Kira. It was so frustrating, but she just wanted to stay in her own world.

I couldn't give up, though, so once she got home I would set up role-play scenarios to mirror the playground. 'Right, Kira, let's get the teddies and the dolls out. We're going to play schools.' I would line them all up and give them the names of children in her class. We'd role-play games of catch, It, and other playground favourites. 'You're it,' Kira would say to one of the dolls. 'Okay, now you have to run and teddy is going to catch you.' We'd play like this happily for about twenty minutes then Kira would start throwing the teddies at the window and kicking the dolls. I never got angry with her, I'd just say gently, 'That's not very nice, is it? Even dolls and teddies have feelings.'

Her behaviour took its toll on me and sometimes I was so frustrated. 'Go to your room, Kira', I'd say gently. Then I'd make a cup of tea, sit down and give myself a good talking to. 'Now listen, Mia,' I'd say. 'She's only a child, you can't give up.' I'd pick myself up, go and find Kira, sit her down and say, 'You need to try to make friends with the other children.' Kira would just stick her fingers in her ears and sing: 'La-la-la-la-la. Not listening!'

The truth was that Kira's self-esteem was so low that she thought she wasn't worthy of friends. As far as Kira was concerned, people hurt and rejected her so she would hurt and reject them first so she didn't have to face it.

It puzzled me that Brody, the other extremely difficult foster child we'd cared for who was a nightmare at home, was popular with everyone. He managed to present a convincing front to the world, and he was loved for it. People still say to me now, 'What happened to that lovely little boy you used to look after?' I grit my teeth and say, 'He's grown up now and living with his family.' Poor Kira just simmered with resentment. She was like a coiled cobra waiting to strike, and everyone steered clear.

Her behaviour was like a teenager's even when she was five years old, so it was hard to remember she was still in the infant school. My job was to try to make people see that she was just a little girl and she needed nurturing just like any other little girl. If I could manage that, Kira might have a chance at integrating. There's an old saying, 'It takes a whole community to raise a child.' And this was never more true than in Kira's case. If I could get the community to see what I could see – that she was just a little girl – then we might have a chance.

It would be a long, hard journey. If the phone went at lunchtime, nine times out of ten it was the school. 'Mrs Marconi, it's Mr Belmarsh here. I need to talk to you about Kira. I'm afraid she has been too disruptive in the classroom. You'll have to take her home.'

I'd go in for meetings to discuss strategies to help Kira, and the school did try really hard. 'We think this might work, Mrs Marconi. [I never had the heart to say that I wasn't married.] 'We've tried to help Kira at playtime, but nothing has worked. We think Kira would be better staying in at lunchtime. She is going to help the teachers.' They would give her little tasks to carry out, but they found her exhausting with her endless demands.

Around 1 p.m. the phone would ring and Mr Belmarsh would say coldly, 'Kira has flooded the toilets.' Or: 'Kira's torn up so-and-so's books and she's hidden the children's lunch boxes all over the school.' She would be reprimanded, of course, but the more attention she got, the more she demanded, and her bad behaviour was all about demanding attention.

'What happened at school today, Kira?' I would ask when I picked her up.

'I hate school. No one at school likes me.'

'That's because they don't know you, darling, and I think you sometimes hurt and upset people too. If you could be kinder to people and not hurt them, you would make friends.' Kira would look blankly at me.

It was frustrating that we were making headway with Kira at home while at school it was two steps forward and three back. It's not unusual for foster children to struggle at school as the environment is too overwhelming for them. They can just about deal with people on a one to one level but trying to cope with twenty-nine other kids in a class, keep teachers happy, keep playground staff happy and try to learn is often too much for kids who have such complex needs.

And so our daily conversations would play out with me trying to find a path for Kira that would help her negotiate the politics of the playground.

As things got worse at school, Kira became very clingy to me at home and very controlling. She was hypervigilant, a clear sign of post-traumatic stress, and she had to know exactly what was happening at all times. Her controlling behaviour was all part of this; it was about her needing to exert some control over her own destiny. She needed to feel powerful, and although I understood what was going on, living with it was extremely tiring.

A typical scenario was this: my sister Rosa would ring. 'Hi, Rosa, how are you? Yes, I'd love to have lunch tomorrow.' If Kira heard me making arrangements to meet anyone, you could bet your life that she would be sent home from school so that I would have to cancel. I lost count of the number of times I was about to head out of the door to meet a friend when the phone would ring and it would be Mr Belmarsh, saying: 'Kira told Mr Smith to fuck off. You need to come and pick her up.'

When I did pick her up she was less than grateful. 'You fucking slag, you whore. I can't stand you,' she'd say. It's always humiliating and a shock when a five-year-old uses that language but I forced myself not to react.

'You need to go to your room when we get home, Kira,' I'd say calmly. 'You can't talk to me like that. You can't talk to anyone like that.' And Kira would spend the rest of the day in her room.

When Kira was about seven she was sent home from school one afternoon and she raced up to her bedroom. She came down for dinner and the table was particularly busy that night. Ruby and Francesca both had friends over and there was a lot of giggling going on. After we'd cleared up, Kira went back to her room. 'She's a bit quiet,' I thought and went to knock on her door. 'What?!' she said. What I saw when I walked in stopped me in my tracks. On the floor were hundreds of pieces of shredded paper. She had taken all her life stories – we'd made about a dozen in all – and ripped them to pieces. Nothing could be saved.

'Kira, what have you done?' I asked as I slid down the bedroom wall in shock. I began to cry. 'Why are you crying?' she said.

'I'm really sad. That's all your life story work. I'm sad that you won't have any memories.' All she said was: 'I'm not.'

Every happy family moment was torn into tiny pieces, all the picnics and parties, birthday celebrations and holidays. I didn't need to be Einstein to work out that however hard we tried, Kira knew she was only a temporary part of our family and felt like an outsider at times. This was her way of showing herself that family wasn't important.

Chapter Five

So that I could have some kind of normal life I had to become secretive myself, whispering whenever I wanted to make an arrangement and making sure that Kira was out of earshot whenever possible. 'Don't say anything in front of Kira,' I told Rosa or Mum if they wanted to meet me.

I longed for the school not to ring in the middle of the day, but it was inevitable and happened at least once a week. Kira was totally disruptive. She ruined other children's work. She would take the food from their lunch boxes and throw it in the bin. She would throw chairs, kick pupils and smash windows. She was like a tiger once she was confined to the classroom.

If she got the chance she would bolt. There was a large field at the side of the school and if she could she would make a run for it. When she did she was more like a wild rabbit running for its life, and with the best will in the world no one was going to catch her.

On these occasions I was called to the school to talk to her. There was never much talking; just the sight of me seemed to soothe her because she knew she would be going home. We often walked home in silence, Kira staring at the ground relieved that she no longer had to endure the loneliness of school. Thoughts were whirling round in my head as I tried to think of something to say that might reach her and help her fit in, but we were three years in. I'd pretty much said everything.

I put myself in her shoes: she was surrounded by hundreds of children at school, but that just compounded her loneliness because she wasn't able to make friends with any of them. She was much happier in her own room by herself. Her bad behaviour was all about communicating this but no one was listening, so in her mind she would just have to try harder to get them to hear.

Most of us have felt lonely at some point in our lives, perhaps entering a party or a new workplace in the wrong frame of mind. You can be in a room full of people yet you hear no voices and see no faces once the anxiety of being alone takes over. That must have been what Kira felt on a daily basis.

I delved back into Kira's early childhood and tried to pinpoint the places where I could fill in the gaps. But it was a black hole; the whole of it was missing! If only she had got to the toddler stage, when you can leave your two-year-old at nursery and they cling to you a bit for reassurance when you turn to leave. You leave them with a favourite toy to comfort them, and when you come back they're waiting patiently on their little chair, watching for your face. Eventually, they realise that it's okay, that you will come back, and before long you have to coax them to leave nursery because they're too happy playing. If Kira had reached that stage in her development it would have been different – we might have had a chance.

When I was studying the psychology of caring, I watched an experiment in which monkeys were deprived of their childhood. Baby monkeys were taken away from their mothers at birth and put in a wire cage next to other baby monkeys, all in similar wire cages. They could see each other but couldn't touch each other and lived alone, with no physical contact with their own species.

In each cage there were two wire tubes – surrogate mothers – about the same size as their real mothers would have been. One tube was wrapped with soft towelling and the other was just naked wire. Milk was fed to the babies from a bottle placed inside the wire tube. Scientists watched to see whether the monkeys favoured the food-dispensing tube or the tube that offered them some comfort. They discovered that the babies clung to the towelling tubes for up to twenty-two hours a day, only leaving when hunger forced them to. When a technician opened the cage to refresh the milk they would desperately try to cling to her, but were brushed away. They had virtually no contact with any living thing and their little faces looked constantly anxious. Not surprisingly, they grew up to be abusive and they had trouble mating.

I thought about trying to explain all this to Mr Belmarsh as a way to explain Kira's behaviour, but even if he understood, what could he do? There were two hundred other children in the school and he was responsible for making sure they got an education. He wasn't a child psychologist.

Mr Belmarsh had no time for Kira because he didn't have any to spare for her, but there was one teacher, Miss Gannon, who was amazing. She was in her fifties and all the kids were scared of her. She was strict but fair, with a tough exterior. She fitted the stereotype of the middle-aged, single-woman teacher. In fact, she was quite similar in appearance to Miss Trunchbull, the headmistress in the film *Matilda*. She wore no make-up, her grey hair was cut into an unforgiving helmet shape, and she sported tweed suits and lace-up brogues. Although the kids would shake when she walked into the room, she took a shine to Kira and Kira liked her.

Miss Gannon was a woman who kept people at arm's length. Perhaps she recognised something in Kira, like my dad, and felt sorry for her, or maybe the challenge of turning Kira around was one she wanted to take on. She didn't say, but I was grateful she was taking an interest.

By the time Kira was seven her lunchtimes were spent helping Miss Gannon organise the classroom and set out the tables. This suited her because she didn't have to make friends, and it suited Miss Gannon because she needed company. It wasn't just the children who didn't like her – the other staff members seemed not to warm to her either. It also really suited me because I didn't have to pick Kira up every lunchtime.

Like all Kira's friendships it came to an abrupt end, in this instance when Kira broke Miss Gannon's arm. The phone went one afternoon and it was Mr Belmarsh. 'I'm afraid there's been a serious incident, Mrs Marconi. Kira threw a chair during her lesson. Miss Gannon tried to restrain her but Kira pushed her. She fell and broke her arm.' I was speechless.

'Why did you throw the chair, Kira?' I asked her when I picked her up. 'I don't know, Mia. I was just cross,' she replied. I wondered if Kira was spending too much time alone with Miss Gannon and that sharing her had become impossible for her.

After that I knew it would kick off. The phone went and it was Mr Belmarsh. 'I've consulted the school governors and Kira is excluded from school until further notice. We are having an emergency meeting to decide what our next step should be.'

Mr Belmarsh was exasperated with Kira, and I think it's safe to say that she was not his favourite pupil. He was tired of fielding complaints from parents and teachers about her.

Chapter Six

Summer holidays are a great chance to recharge, for me and the children. We leave our home for at least a month and it is fantastic to get away with Martin, my kids and the foster kids. After about a week the children begin to calm down and the dramas of their school lives and friends are all forgotten. It becomes about simple pleasures: days at the beach, good food and hanging out with family. Everything and everyone else is dismissed for a while.

Most years we go to Italy, and the year Kira turned eight was no exception, although I also booked a hotel in Tenerife for the last two weeks of the school holidays. I'll never forget the day we flew there. We were all filled with excitement and anticipation, but somehow Kira looked as miserable as ever. I had learnt not to ask her what was wrong because the excitement of the moment would suddenly become negative. It was generally nothing in particular but there was always a nagging fear that there was something serious bothering her. It was much better to ask her in a quiet moment later if she still looked sad, but often she moved on quite quickly and the moment would pass. I wouldn't go so far as to say she got into the spirit of the occasion, but she moved on. I'd learned to stop beating myself up about it. Experience had taught me that if I began talking to Kira when she was unhappy about anything she would get embarrassed and cause a drama. That put everyone else on edge. The truth was that she generally didn't know what was wrong herself.

The flight went without a hitch and it always made me smile watching the kids as their meals arrived on trays. They loved them, even though the food could never be described as gourmet.

When we arrived, the hotel in Tenerife was beautiful and the weather was fantastic, and I knew it was going to be a great holiday.

Kira's birthday is on 1 September, which meant she was never at school to celebrate it. This was a godsend because no one would have come to any birthday party hosted by Kira. We always had a family party for her but I decided I wanted to do something special this year while we were away.

As a family we often spoke about our favourite animals or what we would like to be if we were animals. 'I want to be an elephant,' Francesca would say, and she loved her cuddly elephant. 'Elephants are stupid,' Ruby would add. 'Bears are the best.'

Ruby loved bears and had a large collection of them. We had bedtime storybooks that focused on their favourite animals. *We're Going on a Bear Hunt* was one, and we loved Jill Murphy's elephant books about the Large family, particularly *Five Minutes' Peace*. We would laugh for hours about the antics of Mr and Mrs Large and their Large children, and often created the same scenes at home.

Kira watched and listened and occasionally broke into a smile when we started play-acting. On these occasions I felt lifted, because moments when Kira smiled were few and far between.

She had a favourite book of her own about sea life. It was colourful, bold and visual, and full of fish and sea creatures. It named them all and Kira could name them all too. It became her favourite book and she found the pictures mesmerising. 'Tell me about the stingray, Mia,' Kira would say. 'Why do whales blow water out of their holes, and is it really true that seahorse daddies are the ones who have the babies?'

The dolphin was the most special sea creature to her. We both shared a passion for them. They are beautiful, elegant and friendly, the perfect mammal, really. Kira loved that book and took it with her when we went to Tenerife.

We were flying home the day after Kira's birthday so I wanted to plan something special for her. I was determined that she should have a special memory to take with her. I picked up a bunch of excursion flyers from reception and settled down by the pool to leaf through them. 'Swimming with Dolphins', one flyer advertised. That was it! The perfect birthday treat.

I rushed around while Martin entertained the children, and I managed to get everything organised. I even managed to order an ice-cream cake covered in kiwi fruit. Kiwis were Kira's favourite.

'Wake up, Kira. You're swimming with dolphins today,' I said on her birthday. 'Really?' she asked. 'Yes, really. Happy birthday!' Kira sat there and blinked and could not hide a smile. 'Come on, get your cossie. We're leaving after breakfast.'

I left Martin with the other children. They were going on a trip that day, which meant I could have some one-to-one time with Kira. After breakfast we headed down to the harbour and got on the boat that would take us to see the dolphins. They were in the aqua park, which was about thirty minutes away, and I could tell by the way Kira constantly fiddled with her hair that she was getting excited.

Once we arrived, one of the organisers said: 'Here's a snorkel and a mask, Kira. You get to hug and stroke young Splash here.' And she put a hand on the head of one of the three dolphins in the water. Kira slid into the pool next to Splash, while I slid in beside her. 'Hello, Splash,' she said as she stroked the dolphin's back.

'Now, hold onto Splash's fin, Kira. Not too tight, and just let her pull you along. Let go if she swims too fast.'

Kira looked at me for reassurance. 'Don't worry, I'm right with you,' I said. Splash began to swim away and I could tell that Kira was in seventh heaven.

We were there for almost an hour, and Kira was taught how to make Splash do tricks like jumping through a hoop or doing a back flip. She had her photograph taken hugging and kissing Splash, and she also got picked to take part in the show that the dolphins put on afterwards. In the shop she spent another hour choosing something to buy as a souvenir of her day and eventually settled on a glass dolphin. 'Hurry up,' I said gently. But she refused to be hurried, even though we were starving and anxious to get back to the hotel for her birthday dinner.

It was an amazing experience and, for once, everything went to plan, I thought.

I thought too soon. On the way back the heavens opened and we were soaked in a brief downpour. It was brief, but by the time we got back to the hotel we looked like drowned rats. I laughed it off, but Kira's face was as sullen and dark as any storm cloud.

I put her straight into a lovely warm shower. The others were back and we all got dressed up for dinner. All except Kira. 'I'm wearing my pyjamas. I'm cold,' she said sulkily. 'That's fine, darling,' I said. I knew there was no point arguing because the only result would be heartache and stress, and Kira would still wear her pyjamas.

We all filed into the dining room, with Kira in her PJs. It didn't matter; the dinner was perfect and the ice-cream cake arrived at the table covered with sparklers. It was every child's dream and Kira's eyes gleamed. I think I almost saw her smile, but then I could have imagined it because I so longed for it. 'Happy birthday to you,' we sang, and Kira watched as the sparklers faded. She managed to eat two slices of cake, and although she didn't say anything I knew it was the perfect birthday.

A couple of days after we got home, Kira's new social worker Liz came to visit. She had only met Kira once before, just before we left for our first holiday that summer to Italy.

I had no strong feelings about her either way, other than that she seemed like someone who was just doing her job and wouldn't stay long. During the meeting Liz asked about our holiday. 'We had a wonderful time,' I said.

'And how was your birthday, Kira?'

'It rained!' she wailed.

Chapter Seven

Kira was demanding and draining on the family. My kids are grounded and secure so they didn't need constant attention from me and were happy to help me nurture others, but even they were struggling and were getting fed up and resentful. They'd come to the end of their tether. It was tiring for me trying to keep everyone happy and I went to bed in tears every night. 'I'm exhausted really,' I told my social worker Cathy.

'Maybe we should look at some respite care for you,' she said. I was never keen on respite because it broke continuity for the child. I still resist it because it doesn't feel comfortable. I wouldn't send my own children to a stranger's house, would I? If I needed a break they would go to their nan's or their auntie's house, or they would stay with a school friend. But I had none of these support systems for Kira as no one could cope with her.

'I think you're right. We do need respite if we are going to survive,' I said.

'I know Kira can be like a mini-whirlwind once she gets going.'

'Don't know about a whirlwind; she's a full-on tornado.' We laughed. It was good to make light of the situation, even though it was becoming quite serious.

'Give me a couple of days and I'll come back to you, Mia.'

'Thanks, Cathy. My kids want to have a weekend where they can have their mummy to themselves and be able to go out somewhere without me having to come home.'

Cathy suggested respite with a couple who lived about half an hour from us. John Lipsey and his wife Jackie were prepared to take Kira for the weekend, she said. In fact, they were happy to take her whenever we needed them to.

They had children of their own, and their son Ben was the same age as Kira. It was ideal, and the fact that there were other kids around was good, I thought.

Kira and I went to meet them one Saturday. They lived in a three-storey house in the middle of a terrace on a scruffy estate, but there were children playing out on the street and bikes scattered around on the pavements, which was a good sign. There were plenty of cars parked up but I saw no traffic, so I knew it would be safe.

I confess that the house looked in disrepair but who was I to judge? A carer's ability to care isn't based on the look of their house, I told myself.

The kitchen was chaos, with piles of dirty dishes in the sink and the breakfast things still on the table. My home is no show home but I am quite fastidious about housework. I've learnt over the years that not everyone is as fastidious as me, so I try to concentrate on the person rather than their surroundings.

Jackie pulled a chair out while Kira clung to my side. 'I'll put the kettle on,' she shouted. 'Lovely,' I said. Kira looked round the room, taking everything in. Like my house, there seemed to be people in and out all the time. It was as busy as a doctor's waiting room.

There was a baby in a high chair banging on it with a wooden spoon. Kira looked at her and I was surprised when she broke into a smile. 'Kira seems to love babies,' I explained to Jackie. 'She is really good with them.'

'I always need help with the baby,' she said to Kira, who looked at me for reassurance.

'You'd like to help, wouldn't you, Kira?' I asked. She looked at Jackie and nodded.

I tried not to stare at Jackie but she was as scruffy as her kitchen. Her clothes were unkempt, but she was bubbly. I liked her, I truly did. She made us feel welcome and started chatting to Kira and not me, which I also liked.

After we finished our tea we walked into the front

room, which was just as chaotic. Jackie must have seen the look on my face. 'Oh, sorry,' she giggled. 'That's all my ironing I'm sorting out.' John and Ben were watching a football match on television. They stood up to introduce themselves then sat down and continued to watch the game.

We stayed for an hour then left and got back into the car. On the way home Kira and I began to talk about the Lipseys. 'I like them. I don't mind going to stay there,' she said.

It could be an adventure for her, I thought, and it was only for some weekends. Maybe it would work. I felt slightly elated but kept it to myself. If Kira realised for one minute I was excited about this she would do something to sabotage it. 'It will be fun. I can play with the baby,' she said. 'Okay, well, if you're sure. Not straight away, but maybe in a few weeks' time.'

A month later, when the exhaustion was really getting to me, I phoned Jackie. I would drop Kira at her house on Friday night and she would bring Kira back to my house on Sunday. It worked. I never stayed long when I dropped her off as I had usually been driving for two to three hours because of all the school runs. By the time I got there, all I wanted to do was get home, put my feet up and catch up with the family.

That weekend, while Kira was away, we all relaxed, and I confess it was the most peaceful weekend we'd had since she'd arrived. We spent Saturday at the swimming pool and then had a large family lunch on Sunday. We laughed a lot that weekend and we felt rejuvenated.

On Sunday the doorbell went at about 5 p.m. It was Jackie with Kira. 'Come in, come in,' I said as I hugged Kira. 'I won't stop, Mia. Need to get back. Call me again when you need me.'

'Thanks, I will,' I said. I turned to Kira. 'Did you have a lovely weekend?' I asked.

'Yes,' she said. 'Look at my photo album. John took lots of pictures.' There were pictures of Kira on the swing in their garden, pictures of her doing a jigsaw puzzle, pictures of her playing with the baby. Suddenly, I felt inadequate. She'd only been there for the weekend and she already had a photo album. 'That's really caring,' I thought.

I used the weekend respite facility about five times during that year, and for one week in the summer period when they took Kira camping. Kira was always happy to go and there were never any tantrums or tears. It worked well, gave us a well-needed break and I never had any concerns about her.

Chapter Eight

Since Kira had been living with us she would get the occasional visit from her father. She looked forward to seeing her dad but the feeling wasn't mutual. Plus, Hafeez would never come by himself. He would always bring her half-brothers with him so that he wouldn't have to be on his own with her. For Kira, that meant she could never get the one-to-one contact with him that she craved.

It might have been different if she shared a bond with her brothers, but I felt really uneasy when they were with us because the older one would look at Kira with such undisguised hatred I feared he could really harm her. I had never seen a child deliver such a vicious look and I found it truly disturbing. Consequently, I never took my eyes off them for a minute.

While the boys and Kira bounced on the trampoline, Hafeez would talk to me and I would make sure he had his back to the garden so that I could look over his shoulder.

On one particular occasion he wanted to talk about his affair with Mary.

'She never told me she was pregnant until it was too late,' Hafeez said, unable to say Mary's name. 'Can you imagine the shock I felt?' And I stopped myself from saying, 'Well, you are a grown man, you know the facts of life; you could have taken precautions.'

I knew Mary would have told him she was on the pill, but he knew what she was like – she already had eight children, for goodness sake. He shouldn't have been fooled.

'The minute she brought the baby home she began blackmailing me, asking me for money all the time,' he said, and he told me about the terrible fights they had and how the police were called. 'She kept demanding money from me. She said if I didn't pay her she would tell my wife Sana about the child.' It didn't escape me that he didn't say Kira's name either. Threats were thrown around like hand grenades, but Mary knew she held the trump card.

'I had to pay her as much as I could. I thought she would spend the money on the child but she spent it on alcohol. Why do they drink? Drink is evil,' Hafeez said. He was a Muslim, so he never touched a drop of alcohol and felt quite strongly about it. I bit my tongue swallowing the word 'adultery', which is also against his religion as it is mine. But one of the many things I've learned is that it's a rare person who is able to live their life completely free of hypocrisy, including me.

'She blackmailed me for a year until she got bored of fighting and bored of looking after Kira. Then, just after the child was one, she knocked on our door. I was at work so Sana opened it to find "her" drunk and standing there with the child.

'I can't believe she came to my house drunk!' Hafeez said with his head in his hands. 'She left the baby with my wife. Sana knew nothing about her before. It was a terrible shock for her.'

Mary knew that leaving Kira with Hafeez's wife would cause her an enormous amount of distress. It would be a knife in the heart every time Sana looked at Kira, and Mary knew that. But even worse, it was more rejection for Kira who, after all, was an innocent child caught in the emotional crossfire. However awful her mum was, she was reliant on her, and to be handed over to a stranger must have been devastating. I shivered when I thought what a terrible first couple of years that poor little girl must have had.

Unsurprisingly, social services stepped up their involvement. 'We agreed to take Kira at weekends,' Hafeez said. 'But Mary stopped picking her up on Sunday nights and it would be Monday or Tuesday before she came.' The truth was that Mary's alcohol problem was spiralling out of control and she was becoming more and more chaotic. Kira was the least of her problems.

I listened quietly to Hafeez's story. Whether he was pouring his heart out because of guilt or sorrow or just because he had no one else to talk to, I didn't know, but I sensed it was important that I let him carry on. Each nugget of information was a piece of Kira's jigsaw puzzle in any case, and the more pieces of the puzzle I had, the easier it would be to help her through this mess.

Hafeez stopped his story as he clearly didn't want to relate the awful details, but I knew the full horrors as I'd heard what happened next to Kira from Roz.

She knew that after Kira started nursery school the carers reported that she was an angry little girl prone to sudden outbursts, who would often hit out and spit at staff. She was unsociable and didn't interact with other children. She had, however, finally formed a relationship with a carer to whom she had confided. She told the carer one afternoon that her stepfather Bob had touched her. The child protection team were alerted, as were medical professionals and police officers. She was removed immediately and placed in foster care, where she remained for a few weeks before Hafeez agreed to take her full time.

When Kira began living at their house permanently, Hafeez was working as a night security guard in a large factory while Sana stayed at home and looked after the children. Money was tight, and with an extra mouth to feed it began to get tighter. The whole situation was a pressure cooker waiting to blow.

Six months later, nursery school staff became increasingly worried about Kira's appearance. They reported that she was very tired and was falling asleep as soon as she was dropped off. She fell asleep at every opportunity, wherever she could find a quiet corner. Social services were called again along with all the other agencies attached to Kira's case.

Hafeez was still working nights, and it turned out that once he left for work, Sana would not allow Kira to go to sleep but made her walk up and down the hall while she and her boys slept in lovely comfortable beds. If Kira dared to grab any sleep she would curl up in the corner of the hallway, but woe betide her if Sana got up in the night and discovered her sleeping. She would get a good hiding if she was caught.

By the time Hafeez came home from work they were all having breakfast like nothing had happened.

Sana hated Kira and made no excuses for her actions. She refused to speak to social workers and the only comment she would make was that 'Kira was naughty and that was her punishment.'

Kira was removed immediately on an emergency placement order. It wasn't long before the courts granted social services a full care order and, finally, parental responsibility was taken away.

I thought about her life then. She had never known a hug or a cuddle; there was not a single soul in the world who cared about her except for the nursery school staff, and what could they offer apart from a few words of encouragement? She was starved of love, and boy did it show.

Chapter Nine

I kept trying to help Kira find a place to fit in. Nothing had changed at school; she was never going to conform to their rules and it was unlikely that she ever would. But the one area Kira felt comfortable in was sport. We tried them all – netball, football, tennis, trampolining – as I had a strong desire for Kira to interact; a desire she didn't share. Although she excelled at them, she hated team sports. I finally surrendered when she walked off a football pitch in tears.

'Don't pass the ball to Kira,' one of the kids whispered to the rest of the team. They didn't like her so no one would pass her the ball. She spent the whole match running up and down the wing desperate to do something. 'I'm here,' she would shout, but whoever had the ball would look wildly around for anyone else to pass it to apart from her. She finally snapped, but instead of heading for the changing room she ran. She ran and ran until she couldn't run anymore. I got in the car and went searching for her, and I found her a couple of miles away sitting by the side of the road in the pouring rain. I opened the car door and said nothing. Neither did she. I had pushed her too far.

The fact that she had run so far gave me an idea, though. Always looking for a silver lining, I thought. 'You like running, don't you, Kira?'

'I'm fast. I love it,' she said.

'Well, there's a place called an athletics club where they will let you do nothing but run. You don't have to do it in a team; you can do it by yourself.'

'Really?'

'Yes, really. Would you like to try?'

I took her to the local athletics club and she loved it. She could run and run and not have to have a conversation with another soul. She joined a swimming club too, where she could swim length after length without having to talk. It was the perfect environment as she didn't have to interact with any of the other children.

Although I'd found some outlets for Kira, I was still having endless meetings with social services about her behaviour. Eventually they asked me to seek medical advice, so we attended a children's centre near my home. 'Is Kira the same at home as she is at school?' the doctor asked. 'I mean, is she as aggressive at home as she is at school?'

'She's pretty much the same, although she's worse when she's in a crowd, so school makes her behaviour worse,' I told him.

'Her aggression and problems socialising all point to ADHD – attention deficit hyperactivity disorder,' the doctor told me. 'This is the reason she is having problems concentrating at school, socialising and why she is so impulsive. We're going to prescribe Ritalin. It will help calm her down and she will find life easier.'

I was familiar with Ritalin. When Francesca and Ruby were five and six, I was studying for an advanced qualification in health and social care. I was offered a placement for three months in America, where I studied at various orphanages.

I was quite shocked by the amount of Ritalin that was prescribed in the children's homes, and most of the morning meeting was spent discussing who should have a higher dose. 'Is there any alternative to giving them drugs?' I would chip in occasionally. 'It makes them much calmer,' was the usual response.

Ritalin suppressed their symptoms, but I wondered what would happen to all the anger that was now being chemically coshed. Wouldn't it be better if it all came out and was dealt with now rather than in adulthood, after they stopped taking the drug?

I questioned then whether these children were being labelled because they didn't fit into the appropriate boxes or whether they really had a problem. What I witnessed in the States didn't convince me that Ritalin was some wonder drug that cured unruliness. It lessened the symptoms but I could see no sign of a cure.

I confided in Martin. 'I feel sad that Kira is being prescribed Ritalin because it means that everyone can stop trying to understand her and help her. They can't cure ADHD so she will just be on drugs for ever.'

'Maybe they just realise they have no answers and this is the only thing left,' he said.

'You might be right,' I said. But I wondered what that would mean for her future.

Were these kids any different to the disruptive kids we had at my school in the 1970s, I wondered. Then they were given the naughty label, not the ADHD label. I'm no doctor but I asked myself whether 'energetic' was more appropriate than 'hyperactive'. We are all born with different characteristics. Some of us are introvert, some are extrovert, others outspoken or quiet. Some are sporty or academic, musical or artistic; we're all so different. Was it ADHD that Kira was suffering from or was it the result of a constant battle with her environment? She had been crushed on so many occasions. She had been left isolated, withdrawn and angry. So was she suffering from ADHD or was it the result of the hardship she had endured? No one could give me a definitive answer.

I gave her the Ritalin and waited to see how she changed. It didn't make much difference; she just wasn't as aggressive. Her personality lost its power and she became sedated. I should have felt relieved, but I didn't because it felt so wrong to me that this child was being suppressed with drugs. 'All those feelings have got to come out at some point,' I said to Martin. 'She's going to blow like a volcano one day.'

'Can't they think of anything else?' he asked.

'They just think it's the right thing. But I can't see how. It just seems as though we're delaying dealing with the problem. It just seems like giving a child a tablet so that you can have a peaceful life makes us part of the problem, not part of the solution.'

He nodded, but I knew I had no choice. I had to give her the pills.

Kira did suffer one worrying side-effect: her weight plummeted to a dangerously low level. She had none to spare in the first place – she was a skinny little thing – but she must have lost a stone at least. After a month on Ritalin she became skeletal and looked anorexic. I took her to the doctor. 'I think we should take you off the Ritalin, Kira,' he said quickly.

Within a week she started to put the weight back on.

Doctors felt more tests were necessary, though, so we took her to our nearest children's hospital. The results showed that Kira was a fragile X syndrome carrier, which meant she had a faulty X chromosome.

'Fragile X is a genetic condition that causes a range of developmental problems, learning disabilities and cognitive impairment,' the specialist said. 'The cause could be folic acid deficiency.'

I thought about her mother, whose diet while she was pregnant would have been principally alcohol, and she wouldn't have recognised a broccoli spear or a spinach leaf even if she was concerned about folic acid. 'Can we do anything about it?' I asked.

'There is no cure but this is the reason Kira has limited intellectual function and the reason she's struggling to socialise.

'There is one other thing you should be aware of. Fragile X can be a problem if Kira has children. She will have to seek advice if she gets pregnant and is carrying a boy. If she gives birth to a boy it's likely that he will be severely autistic.'

We needed to manage Kira's condition, I was told. I constantly sat in on meetings listening to the professionals describe how Kira had difficulty concentrating for long periods. 'She's impulsive and acts without thinking,' one would say. 'She's aggressive and shows no empathy,' I heard. Occasionally I would say: 'Isn't that normal for a lot of children? Especially children who have suffered like Kira.' My remarks were often dismissed or I was told, 'Not in the same way Kira is.'

The words most used to describe Kira were hyperactive, boisterous, careless, disruptive … 'Kira is a tomboy,' I would say. No one really knew how to react when I chipped in with these comments. I agreed with their descriptions but I felt these labels were causing more problems for Kira.

'Isn't that what the inclusion policy is all about?' I asked one day. 'I thought the idea of teaching disabled children in mainstream school was so that the labels would disappear and they would become children who couldn't hear as well, walk as well, talk as well, or in Kira's case, concentrate as well as others. Here we are, setting Kira apart by labelling her instead of trying to find a way for her to fit in.' I was determined to stick up for her as nobody else was, but there was an uncomfortable silence, then someone said: 'We have to make sure that we cater for her special needs. Everyone needs to know what they're dealing with.'

I had to admit that I was struggling with Kira, and one night I sat down in front of my computer with a cup of tea and googled 'celebrities with ADHD'. I stared at the screen and a long list came up: Richard Branson, Jim Carrey, Will Smith, Justin Timberlake, Michael Phelps … Will Smith described himself as: 'The fun one who couldn't pay attention.' That wasn't Kira, I thought. Richard Branson said he was dyslexic as well. 'I had no understanding of school work whatsoever. I certainly would have failed IQ tests and it's one of the reasons I left school at fifteen years old,' he said. We were getting closer.

The Olympic champion Michael Phelps caught my eye. He'd won twenty-two Olympic medals for swimming and eighteen of them were gold. I began to smile and looked around for someone to share my find with. Everyone was either doing homework or watching television, so I continued reading by myself.

Michael Phelps partly had his mum to thank for his success. She believed in him when nobody else did, while his teachers complained that he wouldn't sit still or focus on his work. In one magazine she talked about the creative strategies she used to help him with homework. She described how, at age seven, when he began learning to swim, he didn't like the water on his face so she flipped him over and taught him backstroke.

She stressed to him that it was important to be a good sportsman, and she cheered him on at races. He went on to become the most decorated Olympian of all time, breaking thirty-nine world records.

As I read on, there was one major difference between Phelps and Kira. He was brought up in a loving family home and hadn't suffered the type of horrific emotional and physical abuse that Kira had. Still, I thought, there might be something there, and I vowed to keep taking Kira to the pool and the athletics club.

My fantasy was shattered as things at school went from bad to worse. The end result was inevitable –

permanent exclusion. In all fairness the school tried the best they could with the resources they had. Maybe if they'd had an Olympic-size swimming pool or an athletics field things might have worked out differently for Kira, but with thirty children in a class and the teacher at breaking point I'm surprised they held on for so long.

It's almost impossible to expel a child in care because no one wants to inflict another rejection on them, but there are exceptions and Kira was an exception. By the grand old age of ten she was thrown out of school for good.

I had a meeting with social services. 'With no school place or the likelihood of finding a school place that suits Kira's needs, we have to face the only other option, residential care. We highly recommended this option.'

'I agree,' I said quietly, sad that it had come to this.

'Kira will need to move to a family who can care for her long-term.'

I nodded. Officially I was a short-term carer so I knew she would have to move on at some stage. And by now I realised that whatever I did for Kira it was never going to be enough. It was time to see if someone else could succeed where I couldn't.

(Short-term care is a confusing term as Kira had already been with us for six years. But I am approved for short-term care, which means I get calls in a crisis. Realistically, short term can mean days, or years if there's no resolution to the crisis, but it is still classed as short term. Kira should have moved from us by the age of seven to a long-term carer who would be responsible for her until she was eighteen, but because her needs were so complex and we seemed to be offering her a secure home she stayed with us much longer. She was never scheduled to grow up with us, though.)

'I can't do any more to help Kira,' I said to Martin one night, once all the kids had gone to bed. 'I know, love. I've been thinking that for a while.'

'You never said anything.'

'Well, I knew you wouldn't listen and I knew you'd come to the same conclusion eventually.'

I kissed him. I love that man. He knows me so well.

Chapter Ten

I began searching for suitable residential schools for Kira, and so did social services. I wanted better than suitable, though; I wanted perfect, but I knew that perfect was a tall order. I found a place that came pretty close. It was a residential unit in Hampshire that specialised in teaching children on the autistic spectrum. I worked really hard to get the funding, which came from three different sources. The grounds were amazing, the class sizes were small and I thought she could be happy there. The children all received daily therapeutic input and part of the therapy was riding horses. I knew Kira would love that. There was a mixture of children ranging in age from eleven to sixteen. The rooms were pleasant and the grounds were magnificent. Social services took a look and agreed that it was ideal, but now we had to convince Kira.

It had been a wet summer, but on this particular afternoon the sun was shining through the kitchen window, which always brought a smile to my face. 'Kira!' I called upstairs to her. 'I need to talk to you about something.'

'Okay,' she called down, and before long she plodded down the stairs.

She walked into the kitchen, and I looked at her unruly mop of hair and her scruffy tracksuit bottoms. 'What?' she said.

'Nothing. I was wondering whether I would ever see you wear a skirt.'

'Never!' she replied. I laughed.

'You know how you can't go back to school?' I began. 'And you know that the law says you do need to have some kind of an education? Well, we've found this fantastic place where you don't have to have lessons like you had before. The classes are really small, there will be other children there like you, but the best thing is that they teach you how to ride a horse.'

'Really?' she said, not quite believing what she'd heard. 'I like the sound of that.'

'You'll be good at riding because you love sports,' I said. 'Because it's quite far away you'll have to live there, but you can still think of us as your family. You'll be moving to a new family too. One that will look after you until you're old enough to look after yourself. Remember we talked about that a while back? But you can write and visit, and we'll always be here.'

She seemed to accept and be happy with the arrangement. I said, just so that she was clear, 'You won't be living with us anymore. Another family will support you through school.'

She just shrugged, but I wondered what would happen once she had really taken it in.

Social services needed to find a long-term carer who could support her through the next chapter of her life. The carer would need to be close to her new school. It was never going to be an easy search, but it was made slightly easier because Kira was a girl. Boys are far harder to place. Eventually they found Lin, a single lady who had a teenage son.

'She will be able to deal with Kira's complex needs,' Kira's social worker Liz told me. 'She will live there during the holidays, but will spend the rest of the time at school.'

I met Lin a handful of times and warmed to her. She was middle-aged, with a kind face, but more importantly, she seemed committed. Kira visited her with Liz. Lin lived in the countryside in Hampshire, and at the bottom of her garden was a field that was home to several horses. It seemed like fate.

It was a very well-planned move. We had photographs of the school, we visited Lin, we set up meetings and Kira was excited. Although she didn't show it, I could tell by the questions she was asking that it was something she wanted.

'How often will I be able to ride the horses? Will I be able to ride the horses at Lin's or can I only stroke them? Will my room be bigger at Lin's? Will I have my own room at school?'

It was a new chapter for her, but the reality of moving from the only loving family she had known, the only family that had stood by her no matter what happened, the family that still loved her despite the fact she could explode like a land-mine and cause the same amount of devastation, had not yet registered with her. If she had taken it on board she had not recognised it, or if she had she had buried it deep and wasn't ready to contemplate what it really meant. I was under no illusion that reality would hit home as soon as she realised I wasn't picking her up, and I wondered what she would do.

We prepared Kira well for the move. 'You're going to love spending time with the horses, aren't you?' I said.

'They have really soft noses, like velvet. I like it when they push their noses into your arm,' she told me.

'Your room at the school looks really comfortable. Make sure you take lots of your toys.' And I bought her a stuffed horse and a poster of a horse to take with her.

I was excited for her because I felt this was the best place she could be in. I had no doubt that they could look after her and cater for her special needs, and I was confident they would bring out the best in her. I was excited in the way any mother would be if her child was going off to university and it was the best you could find, a perfect fit for them. This was Oxford or Cambridge for Kira.

We had a family party the weekend before she left. She came with me to choose the food and we got a cake. We all bought her little gifts: a diary and a writing paper set with envelopes and a pen, photo albums and she chose a quilt set for her bed.

We hired a bouncy castle with a big slide, which the kids played on all day. We played music, danced, ate and all spoke with great excitement for Kira's benefit, but deep down I was sad, very sad. 'I feel like I've rejected and abandoned Kira,' I told Mum.

'Don't be daft,' she said.

'But we're her only family,' I continued. 'She's been with us for most of her childhood. What kind of person would I be if I didn't feel something? It's like my own child is leaving home prematurely.'

'You'd be dead from the waist up if you felt nothing,' Mum reassured me, 'but you'll all adjust. You know you will. And really, it is the best thing for her.'

'Is it?' I wondered.

I convinced myself that Mum was right but I still felt sad. Realistically, there was no other option and it was out of our hands. The family rallied round and everybody supported me unconditionally because, after all, that's what families do, isn't it?

The morning arrived when Kira was due to leave to start her new life with Lin, and all was going smoothly. My children were excited and so was Kira. It was Sunday and I shouted upstairs for her to hurry down to breakfast. 'It's a full English!' I said. The whole family were waiting and we'd made the table look really inviting with pots of tea, toast and jam, juice and anything else we could find.

'Kira!' I shouted for the third time. 'It's getting cold!' Everyone was trying not to get impatient, but just before they started to really moan Kira walked into the kitchen staring at the floor. I looked at her and my mouth fell open. She had cut all her hair off.

We all looked at each other but no one said anything, because we knew that if we made a fuss she would flip and that would be the perfect breakfast ruined. We managed to ignore her hair, although she had really hacked great chunks off it. After we'd cleared away the table I asked: 'Why did you cut your hair off?'

'I didn't,' she said.

'I'll ask Lin to take you to the hairdresser to get it tidied up.' She said nothing.

Lin arrived at lunchtime and we loaded the car. The whole family helped. It was a new chapter for Kira and she knew we would remain in contact. We already had a lunch date scheduled.

I loved Kira – she almost felt like one of my own children – but I also knew that if she stayed much longer we might buckle under the strain of her constant demands. I was exhausted by this stage and in desperate need of a rest.

A little over a year earlier I'd had another baby, Lucia. By the time Kira was preparing to leave us, Lucia was toddling and I was desperate to spend some uninterrupted time with her.

The following day I got into my routine of school runs. After I got back I was getting ready to feed Lucia and have a cuddle when there was a knock on the door. 'Who is that?' I wondered. I opened it and there was Kira with her suitcase and stuffed horse. Lin stood behind her. 'Sorry, Mia,' Lin mumbled, 'I just can't do this.' Kira was frozen solid, looking at the ground for comfort.

There was silence. No one knew what to say but the awkwardness was broken when Lucia put her arms up to Kira, and Kira picked her up. I marvelled briefly at how great Kira was with babies. 'Come in for a cup of tea, Lin,' I said. Why tea would help on this occasion, I had no idea.

'No thank you, Mia,' Lin replied, looking slightly embarrassed. Her look was more than just embarrassed: it was full of pity. She felt sorry for me. I held her gaze for a split second then she turned and walked away without even saying goodbye to Kira.

I just stood there in silence. My legs felt so heavy I couldn't lift my feet. I was in shock. Months of preparation had been destroyed in just twenty-four hours. Kira walked past me with Lucia in her arms, behaving as though she had just returned from school. Lin might not have wanted a cup of tea but I did. I put the kettle on and gave Kira a cuddle. 'What happened?' I asked.

'Nothing. I didn't do anything,' she said, and just carried on as normal.

'Well, you must have done something.'

'I never did anything. I don't know what she's talking about.'

All I could say was, 'Well, we'll get your hair sorted out today.' And later on I took her to the hair-dresser, who cut her hair into a bob.

I waited for social services to contact me to let me know why Lin had brought her back, but Lin refused to talk to them or me. The only explanation Kira gave – which I didn't hear until some years later – was that Lin had asked her not to go into her son's room, and she had disobeyed. I can only assume it was more serious than that. Kira did have sexualised behaviour, but perhaps the reality of it terrified Lin. Perhaps Kira just didn't want to stay there so she did the one thing she knew would freak Lin out, and her plan worked.

Chapter Eleven

This setback did not mean that Kira's school plans were changed. She would still go to the school, but it would now be her permanent home. We would be able to visit her there. 'After a year, she will probably be able to go on holiday with you,' the school told us. And she would be allowed to visit us, but not for six months. No weekend contact was allowed at first because staff said it unsettled the children too much. She had to stay there so that she could find her feet.

We were allowed to write to her and have weekly telephone contact, but that was it. Literacy was never Kira's strongest subject but what she did write was positive: 'I'm going horse riding. I'm being really good at school. I'm looking forward to seeing you.'

She seemed to settle, but the minute she began to come to terms with the fact that the school was her new family, all hell broke loose. In desperation, the school phoned me to tell me that she kept going into the other children's bedrooms and taking their things. She was hitting the other kids, being disruptive in class and smashing things up. She was just being Kira.

The other kids there were all in the same boat. None of them had families they could go back to either, although some had long-term carers. I could only assume that she thought that if she behaved badly enough they would send her back to live with us, but we'd already accepted another foster child so there was no room for Kira.

Then suddenly her phone calls stopped and her letters too. No one needed to inform me of anything as I was no longer her official carer, but I found out that Kira had been moved. I had no idea where and for a year I tried to discover where she was. Each time I saw a social worker I would ask, 'Any idea where Kira is?' They would promise to come back to me, but the pressures of the job would take over, they had other fires to fight and Kira would be forgotten. Life got busy again, but in quiet moments I would worry about her. Where was she? Who was looking after her? Was she happy?

Eventually, a social worker told me she'd been moved to a school in the north of England that provided specialist services for children, like Kira, who had suffered sexual abuse.

I wrote to her and she replied. I had a few telephone conversations with her, but then I got a chilling call from social services: 'Hi, Mia. This is a bit awkward. Kira's key worker has put in a complaint about you, saying that every time Kira came off the telephone she was upset.'

'I can't think why,' I said.

'I'm afraid telephone contact will have to stop and we'll be in touch with the details.'

I didn't want Kira to feel abandoned so I continued to write to her and send her gifts. I sent her an Easter bunny at Easter, and a dressing gown and gifts on her birthday. But I stopped receiving letters from her.

I consoled myself with the fact that she had letter-box contact with her siblings – not Hafeez's sons, but Mary's children. Social services also set up sibling groups for her so that she could have contact with her half-brothers and sisters. This happened once a year, and at those meetings Kira would find out what was happening in their lives. For some reason, although her siblings were all placed on the at-risk register, they stayed with their parents. As a result they weren't much better off than Kira.

The only communication I had with social services about her during this period was after the complaint from the key worker. 'Her key worker said Kira was crying because in the phone call you upset her about her family,' they told me eventually. I thought back to the last conversation I'd had with her, which was when she was fourteen. 'I'm really fed up,' she'd said. 'Nothing is going right for me.

My brother's in prison, my other brother's had a mental breakdown. My sister's had another baby and she can't look after the two she's already got.'

I said to her: 'Why are you worrying about what all your family are doing, Kira? Worry about what you're doing in your life. It's out of your control and there's nothing you can do about it. Try to surround yourself with positive things.'

Understandably, she was sobbing and sobbing after the phone call because she'd voiced concerns about her family that she hadn't voiced before. Crying is a cathartic process; how many of us don't feel better after a good cry? It's a release and it helps you let go of all sorts of troubles and problems, but her key worker didn't see it like that. 'I'm upset about my family,' she'd wailed when she was asked, and her key worker put two and two together and came up with five.

No one investigated exactly what had gone on, but social services acted and told me that if I wanted to speak to Kira again I would have to sign a contract. 'If you want me to sign a contract, let's have a meeting to discuss what we should put in it,' I said, but I heard nothing after that.

This was a minor incident on social services' radar. As far as they were concerned Kira was no longer in my care, so I didn't need to be involved.

* * *

Two years went by before Kira reached sixteen, left the school and went to live with a foster carer called Penny in Hove on the south coast. It would have made sense for her to come back to live with me, but social services hadn't contacted me because I already had the maximum number of children I could take. With a bit of forward planning it could have been organised for Kira to spend the last of her teenage years here, but she was probably on her third or fourth social worker, who would not have realised the significance of the years she'd spent with us.

One day, completely out of the blue the phone rang and it was Kira. I was delighted to hear from her but they were not happy calls. 'I hate it at Penny's,' she said during one of them.

'Why?'

'I just do.'

'Well, there must be a reason.'

'I just hate it.'

Then after a while the calls stopped and I heard nothing for eighteen months.

There are many foster carers who can provide the love and care that I can, but we're talking about people, and dealing with people with human emotions is not like rehousing stray dogs. However difficult it had been while Kira lived with us, she had forged an attachment to us and that was no mean feat. It was forged millimetre by millimetre, as Kira learned to trust us. To expect her to drop all that and start again was an enormous thing to ask. She just couldn't do it.

While Kira lived at Penny's she went to book-keeping college and gained a minor qualification. She left Penny's at the age of eighteen, but never managed to hold down a permanent job. She got the sack from most places she worked.

I heard nothing from her again until she was nineteen. It was a quiet Sunday afternoon and we'd just finished lunch when the doorbell rang. I opened the door and Kira was standing there. 'Hello, Mia,' she said.

'Oh my God, Kira! I can't believe it,' I said, and gave her a huge hug. 'I'm so happy to see you.'

Kira gave me a big smile. It wasn't like the smiles she used to give that were really just for our benefit; this was a genuine 'I'm really pleased to see you' smile. Within seconds, all the other kids crowded round. Lucia was nine by this time, and Alfie and Isabella were eleven. Francesca and Ruby weren't there because by now they were in their late teens and were out with their boyfriends.

Kira began to talk: 'It took me four hours to find you because I couldn't really remember where you lived.' She'd only spent a few months at this new house after we'd moved, when she was eleven, to a bigger place. 'I knew your address but you know I can't read a map,' she continued, 'and I didn't want to ask anyone directions, so I went back to my old school to try and retrace my footsteps. I took so many wrong turns but I just walked back to the school and started again until I got it right.

'I remember every single thing that happened when I was with you, Mia,' she said. 'I remember what colour the wallpaper was in your old house. I remember what perfume you wore. I remember when Jack and Jill had puppies, and I remember the names we gave them all. And I remember it rained on my eighth birthday.'

'You were a nightmare that day,' I laughed, and she laughed too.

We talked for three hours and she told me that she had never received the gifts I sent to her. 'I could see them in the office, but I wasn't allowed them. They said the other kids would get jealous if I was given them,' she said. 'And anyway, a few times they did give them to me but the other kids destroyed them.'

After a pause, she said, 'Sana died. She got cancer.'

'That's sad,' I said.

'My brother said it was my fault.'

'Well, it wasn't,' I told her, and gave her another hug.

She filled me in on her life in Hove, and I heard grim details about a relationship she'd had with a man twenty years her senior. He was no better than a paedophile and had locked her in his flat. He bought her clothes and gifts in exchange for sex and controlled her every move for a year, but eventually she managed to escape. 'Don't cry, Mia,' she said, as I couldn't stop the tears. 'I got away and I never have to see him again.' Then she said quietly, looking at the floor: 'You were the only family I ever knew and I don't want to lose you again.'

'You won't, darling,' I reassured her, and she allowed herself another smile.

Later, she sent me an email that brought me to tears. It said: 'Your family showed me unconditional love, the only family that ever has. You are the only mum I've ever known, and I will always think of you as a mum for as long as I live.

'The most difficult time in my life was when we lost contact. I felt so lost and scared. It was hard for me to cope then. I don't want to be on my own anymore.'

I wrote back: 'You don't need to worry. We will always be your family and will be there whenever you need us.'

'THANK YOU! :)', came her reply.

Chapter Twelve

Social services found her a place to live that wasn't too far from us. It was a stark place with nothing in it and very few home comforts. 'It's lovely, Kira,' I lied, and then I saw something on the windowsill. It was her glass dolphin. 'Oh my God, you kept it!'

'I always loved it,' she said.

'But you smashed everything else.'

'That birthday was the best birthday I ever had.'

'Bloody hell, Kira. You could have said so at the time,' I said, and we both laughed.

We began to see each other regularly, and although Kira was struggling to hold down a job I was so proud that she hadn't turned to prostitution or started taking drugs to escape. She was really strong and stayed true to herself, and that took tremendous willpower for someone in her situation.

But Kira being Kira, there was always a drama waiting around the corner. About a year after she was back in our lives she called me. It wasn't unusual, as we talked and met regularly. 'The police want to see me,' she said.

'Why?' I asked.

'I don't know. They wouldn't say. They said I'm not in trouble but they want me to go to the station and talk to them. I'm going now. I'll come and see you when I get back.'

'Okay,' I said, and for the next few hours I felt anxious, wondering what on earth had happened.

When Kira finally knocked on my door we sat at the kitchen table and she looked ashen. 'Remember John and Jackie Lipsey?' she asked. 'He's been arrested. Apparently he's a paedophile.'

'Oh my God. Did he ever touch you?'

'No, but he had a naked photograph of me on his computer.'

'How did he get that?'

'Hidden camera in the bathroom.'

'How did the police find out?'

'He tried to kill himself and left a note giving details of his sex offences. My name was on the note but he never touched me.'

'Do you promise?'

'I promise.'

We talked at length about him but Kira said there were no clues as to what he was up to. We were both sickened though, and we talked about the number of visits he would have had from social workers and health visitors. We wondered how no one had picked up on anything, including myself. I was devastated to think that none of us had noticed even the smallest clue. But he was obviously very clever and hid his tracks.

Like me, Kira was shocked. I had met John a few times and had neither liked nor disliked him. I began to look back and the only thing that made me feel uncomfortable was the memory albums full of photos that he had taken. I'd felt inadequate then but I realised now that it was a clever way for him to hide what he was up to. Kira would never question him taking photos, and if she'd said to me, 'John keeps taking photos of me,' I wouldn't have thought to question her because the photos were there for us all to see.

There was a trial and he was sent to prison for twenty years for raping an eight-year-old girl and sexually assaulting numerous others. I have no idea what happened to Jackie but she wasn't arrested.

I began to talk to Kira about the years, particularly the really difficult years, when I needed respite, and I asked her why she was so disruptive. She said: 'They were the happiest days of my life but I didn't realise it. I can't explain why, but what you gave me wasn't enough for me then and there was nothing you could have done to change that. I don't know what I did want, but you've been the only mother figure in the whole of my life and the only one I look up to. I don't know what I would have done without you.'

This was the second time she'd said she considered me to be her mother and I began to trust that she meant it. I felt my shoulders drop, I felt light-headed with happiness, and years of anxiety about whether I had done the right thing for Kira melted away. Who knows how it would have turned out if she had stayed here. She might have been as difficult as ever. Now, though, she had found some peace in her life; she knew what a family was and she was looking forward to the future. She would have her ups and downs, but she knew we would be there for her. Finally, she had accepted us as a family she could trust.

Moving Memoirs

Stories of hope, courage and the power of love…

If you loved this book, then you will love our
Moving Memoirs eNewsletter

Sign up to…

- Be the first to hear about new books
- Get sneak previews from your favourite authors
- Read exclusive interviews
- Be entered into our monthly prize draw to win one
of our latest releases before it's even hit the shops!

Sign up at

www.moving-memoirs.com

Harper True.
Time to be inspired

Write for us

Do you have a true life story of your own?

Whether you think it will inspire us, move us, make us laugh or make us cry, we want to hear from you.

To find out more, visit

www.harpertrue.com or send your ideas to **harpertrue@harpercollins.co.uk** and soon you could be a published author.